ASPCA

PET CARE GUIDES FOR KIDS

HAMSTER

Mark Evans

DK

A DK PUBLISHING BOOK

Project Editor Liza Bruml
Art Editor Jane Tetzlaff
Editor Miriam Farbey
Photographer Paul Bricknell
Illustrator Malcolm McGregor
U.S. Editor B. Alison Weir
ASPCA Consultant Stephen Zawistowski, Ph.D.

First American Edition, 1993
4 6 8 10 9 7 5

Published in the United States by
DK Publishing Inc., 95 Madison Avenue
New York, New York 10016

Library of Congress Cataloging-in-Publication Data
Evans, Mark, 1962-
    Hamster / by Mark Evans : foreword by Roger Caras — 1st American
ed.
        p. cm. — (ASPCA pet care guides for kids)
    Includes index.
    Summary: Provides instructions for choosing, feeding, grooming,
and breeding hamsters.
    ISBN 1-56458-223-X
    1. Hamsters as pets—Juvenile literature.   [1. Hamsters.]
1. Title.   II. Series.
SF459.H3E93 1993
636'.93233—dc20
                                                    92-53475
                                                    CIP
                                                    AC

Models: Tony Arthurs, Emma Aubyn, Amara Clark, Martin Cooles,
Matthew Cummins, Arron Daubney, Suzanne Drake, Lee-Anne
Edwards, Alexandra Harris, Osman Hasan, Cetin Kana, Yewkwan
Mo, Deidre O'Gorman, Deborah Olivera, Emma Scott

Dorling Kindersley would like to thank David Baglin of the British
Hamster Association, PO Box 825, Sheffield S17 3RU for supplying
hamsters for photography; Hamar Acrylics Ltd for making the
perspex tanks; D J Wire for the cages; Supreme Pet Foods Ltd. for
providing dried food; Salvo Tomasselli for the world map, and
Lynn Bresler for the index.

Picture credits: Oxford Scientific Films/G I Bernard p. 13 tr;
Philip Lovell of Oxford Scientific Films Ltd. pp. 12-13 c

Color reproduction by Colourscan, Singapore
Printed and bound in Italy by Arnoldo Mondadori, Verona

Foreword

Hamsters are busy little creatures whose day's work never seems to be done. They run in all directions, they dig things up, then bury their treasures again as fast as they can. All of this activity uses energy and that means that they need food of the right kind and clean drinking water, too. Hamsters try to be neat, but they can't clean their own cages. We are needed to do that job for them. Hamsters teach us a good lesson—what it is like to be needed.

Roger Caras
ASPCA President

Note to parents

This book teaches your child how to be a caring and responsible pet owner. But remember, your child must have your help and guidance in every aspect of day-to-day pet care. Don't let your child have a hamster unless you are sure that your family has the time and resources to care for it properly—for the whole of its life.

Contents

Introduction

The first step to becoming a good hamster owner is to choose the right number and kind of pets. A Syrian hamster must live alone, but you can keep two dwarf or Chinese hamsters together. A hamster with short hair is easiest to care for. You will need special things to care for your pet, and a cage for it to live in. You will have to look after it every day. Not just to start with, but for the whole of its life.

Shopping basket full of equipment you will need

Understanding your pet

You should get to know your hamster very well. If you handle it as much as you can, it will quickly learn to trust you. Watch your hamster carefully. You will soon understand the fascinating things it does.

You can feed your hamster food from your hand

You will need to clean your hamster's cage regularly

Caring for your pet

You will only be your pet's best friend if you care for it properly. You will need to make sure it eats the right foods, always has water, and has plenty of exercise every day.

Things to do with your pet

A hamster is very active. You must play with your pet at least once a day. If you keep your pet busy, you will show everyone that you are a good hamster owner.

You can link cages together to make a hamster wonderland

People to help

The best hamster owner always tries to find out more about her pet. You can ask your veterinarian how to keep your hamster happy and healthy.

You will need to visit your veterinarian regularly

Your pet will become part of your family

Ask a grown-up

When you see this sign, you should ask an adult to help you.

New family member

Your hamster will be a special part of your family. Everyone will want to pet it and be interested in what it does. You can also introduce it to your friends that like animals.

Things to remember

When you keep a hamster, there are some important rules that you must always follow:

Wash your hands after petting or playing with your hamster, and after cleaning its cage.

Don't kiss your hamster.

If your hamster is sleeping or hiding, don't annoy it.

Never tease your hamster.

Do not give your hamster food from your plate.

Never, ever hit your hamster.

What is a hamster?

A hamster is a small rodent that is most active at night. A rodent has very sharp front teeth that never stop growing. They are used for gnawing. Rodents belong to a group of animals called mammals. All mammals have warm blood and a hairy body. When they are very young, they drink milk from their mothers.

Little athlete

A hamster is nimble and energetic. In the wild, it runs as far as five miles (eight kilometers) at night in search of food. It is a very good climber, scrambling over anything in its path. It can bend its body to squeeze through holes and tunnels.

Wide lips

Nostrils

Long whiskers bristle out to feel

Small front leg

Belly has soft hair

Round, pink nipple

Large back leg

Baggy skin helps hamster to turn in tight tunnels

Front paw with five claws is used for digging

Underneath your hamster

A hamster has a big stomach where tough plant food is digested. Look very closely at the belly and you will see pink nipples. Some hamsters have as many as 16! A mother hamster's nipples are sucked for milk by her babies.

Alert ear detects faint sounds

Hamsters see best in dim light

Nose always twitches

Large mouth has room for 16 teeth

Whiskers sense danger around the face

Super night senses

A hamster usually sleeps during the day and is awake at night. It needs keen senses to help it find its way in the dark. A hamster's ears can hear faint sounds. Its nose picks up weak smells. It uses its fine, long whiskers to feel for obstacles.

A closer look at your hamster

The large flap funnels soft sounds into the ear

Pointed front teeth are kept sharp by gnawing

Cheek pouches are used to carry food. They puff out to hold large amounts

Front paws are used like tiny hands to hold food and fill the cheek pouches

Five toes on the back foot are used for grooming

Furry coat protects the hamster from harsh weather

Toes give the hamster a good grip

Stumpy tail

Life in the wild

A wild Syrian hamster lives deep underground in a home called a burrow. Some kinds of hamster dig their own burrows. Other kinds live in the old burrows of other small animals. A hamster stays in its burrow during the day. It will fight off any intruders. When the sun goes down, it leaves the burrow to search for food while it is dark and cool.

Tunnel is the same width as the hamster

Vertical escape tunnel leads straight up to the surface

Larder is used to store food

Babies sleep in nesting chamber

Bathroom

Burrowing behavior

A hamster can dig a tunnel very quickly. It uses its front paws to scoop out the earth and its back feet to kick the soil out of the way. The deepest tunnels are dug in winter so the hamster can shelter far away from cold weather. Some tunnels may be as long as 11 yards (10 meters). The hamster may close a tunnel by pulling a stone over the entrance hole.

Dry, rocky ground

Entrance tunnel slopes down from the surface

Small desert dweller

The Syrian hamster lives in the rocky Syrian desert. It stays in its burrow most of the day to protect itself from the heat. At night, it comes to the surface and travels long distances to find food.

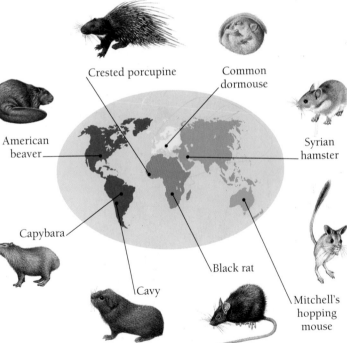

Crested porcupine

Common dormouse

American beaver

Syrian hamster

Capybara

Cavy

Black rat

Mitchell's hopping mouse

A worldwide family

Hamsters are members of a group of animals called rodents. Rodents live all over the world. The group includes tiny mice as well as large animals such as the South American capybara. The cavy, the wild relative of the pet guinea pig, is also a rodent.

Types of hamsters

Many types of hamsters live in the wild. Only a few types are kept as pets. The most common pet hamster is the Syrian hamster. People domesticated dogs and cats many thousands of years ago. The Syrian hamster has only been tamed since about 1940. The smaller Siberian, Djungarian, Chinese, and Roborovsky's hamsters have only recently been kept as pets.

Fine, black line from ears to tail

Black eyes

Furry coat helps keep hamster warm on icy ground

Short, dense fur

Rounded ears

Silver whiskers

Long legs

The Siberian (Winter white)
Siberian hamsters come from the cold north of Asia, where it often snows. Their fur turns white in winter so they are hidden from enemies against the snow.

The Djungarian
Djungarian hamsters are often friendly; even wild ones are not afraid of people. Both Djungarians and Siberians like to live in pairs. They are so small that they are often called dwarfs. They are also known as Russians.

The Roborovsky's hamster
The Roborovsky's hamster is the smallest dwarf hamster kept as a pet. It comes from sandy, desert areas in Mongolia and China.

Black stripe runs down back

Grayish-brown coat

Long, thin tail

Black-tipped ear is small

Narrow body can squeeze through tiny gaps

The Chinese hamster

The Chinese hamster is about the size of a mouse. It is one of a group of hamsters sometimes called Pygmy. In the wild, Chinese hamsters often attack one another. They make their homes in rock crevices or in a burrow.

The Syrian hamster

The big Syrian hamster is one of a group of hamsters called "golden" because of their fur color. In the wild, they are fierce and fight one another.

Shiny, golden fur

Ear is lined with very fine hairs

Plump, round body

Different types of wild hamsters

The mouselike hamster has no cheek pouches and a very long tail.

The common hamster is the largest of all wild hamsters.

The striped hamster has a black stripe down its back.

The gray hamster has large pouches and hoards huge stores of grains.

The ratlike hamster has large pouches.

15

All colors and sizes

The first people to keep hamsters as pets noticed that some hamsters were born with unexpected features. Some had unusual fur colors. Others had new coat markings or hairstyles. By choosing which hamsters had babies, the pet owners made different types, or breeds. New breeds are still being bred today.

Smooth coat is honey-colored

Shaggy coat is brown

Shiny coat is almost white

Black-eyed cream Syrian

Blue mink Syrian

Ivory Syrian

One-color coat

Pet hamsters that are almost all one color are called "self" types. There are many colors, including ivory and blue mink.

Multi-colored coats

Hamsters can have as many as three colors in their coats. The pearl Siberian has two colors, white and gray. The tortoiseshell Syrian has three colors, including yellow and white. If you look closely you will see that the cinnamon Syrian also has three colors: white, orange, and a gray undercoat.

Orange back

White patch

Yellow patch

Brown patch

Tortoiseshell Syrian

Gray face / Pearl Siberian

White arch

White arch

Cinnamon Syrian

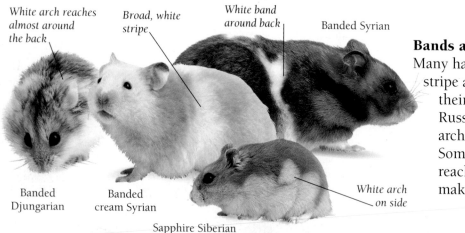

White arch reaches almost around the back

Broad, white stripe

White band around back

Banded Syrian

Bands and arches

Many hamsters have a white stripe around the middle of their body, called a band. Russians have white arches down their sides. Sometimes the arch can reach around the back to make a band.

Banded Djungarian

Banded cream Syrian

White arch on side

Sapphire Siberian

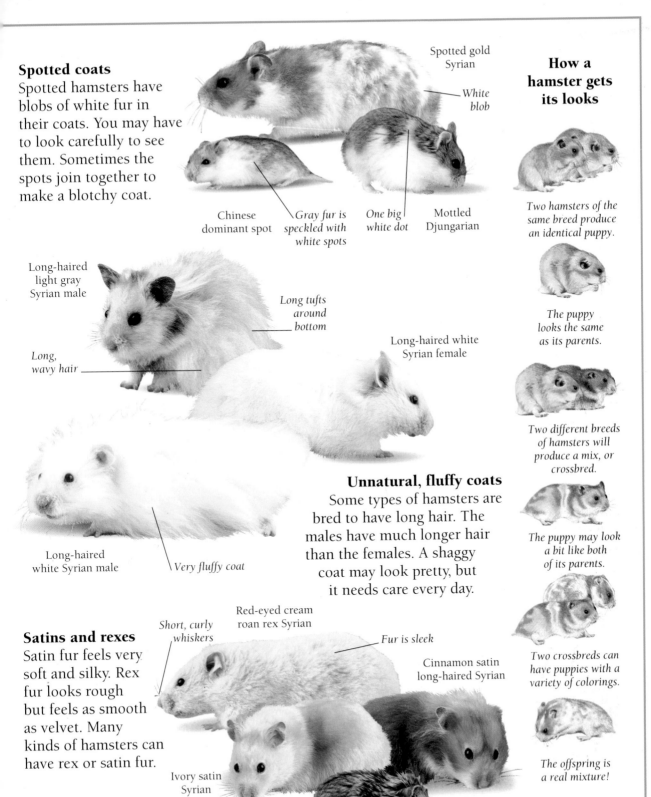

Spotted coats

Spotted hamsters have blobs of white fur in their coats. You may have to look carefully to see them. Sometimes the spots join together to make a blotchy coat.

Spotted gold Syrian

White blob

Chinese dominant spot

Gray fur is speckled with white spots

One big white dot

Mottled Djungarian

Long-haired light gray Syrian male

Long tufts around bottom

Long, wavy hair

Long-haired white Syrian female

Long-haired white Syrian male

Very fluffy coat

Unnatural, fluffy coats

Some types of hamsters are bred to have long hair. The males have much longer hair than the females. A shaggy coat may look pretty, but it needs care every day.

Satins and rexes

Satin fur feels very soft and silky. Rex fur looks rough but feels as smooth as velvet. Many kinds of hamsters can have rex or satin fur.

Short, curly whiskers

Red-eyed cream roan rex Syrian

Fur is sleek

Cinnamon satin long-haired Syrian

Ivory satin Syrian

Smooth satin coat looks very greasy

Normal satin Djungarian

How a hamster gets its looks

Two hamsters of the same breed produce an identical puppy.

The puppy looks the same as its parents.

Two different breeds of hamsters will produce a mix, or crossbred.

The puppy may look a bit like both of its parents.

Two crossbreds can have puppies with a variety of colorings.

The offspring is a real mixture!

Your hamster's home

Buy a large, secure cage for your pet. Make or buy a sleeping box and exercise equipment. Get a food bowl and water bottle. Stock up with food, litter, and bedding. Nothing for the cage should be plastic because hamsters gnaw everything. Put the cage in a safe place, but not in your bedroom because your pet may keep you awake at night.

Thick bars can't be gnawed through

Horizontal bars for hamster to climb

The hamster cage
Look at the measurements in the picture. The cage should be at least this big. The bars must be less than one half inch (one centimeter) apart, because Chinese and dwarf hamsters can squeeze through small gaps. The door must lock firmly.

Side slides up so box can be cleaned

Sleeping box
The sleeping box should have an entrance hole and smaller holes to let in fresh air.

Breathing holes

Burrowing and bedding
You need plain paper to line the tray. Buy untreated soft wood shavings for your hamster to burrow in. Get some shredded paper, paper towel, and hay for bedding.

Lining paper

Bin to store shavings

Scoop

Shredded paper

Paper towel

Soft wood shavings

Hay

Toilet tray and litter

Look for an old tin lid to use as a toilet tray. Get sand or cat litter to put in the tray.

Toilet tray

Cat litter pellets

Fine sand

Gnawing log

Find an untreated fruit tree branch for your hamster to gnaw. Gnawing helps keep its teeth healthy.

Food and bowls

Buy a sturdy bowl, hamster food (see p. 26), and a storage container. You will also need fresh food.

Dry food

Food bowl

Carrots

Storage container

Where to put the cage

Keep the cage away from any drafts.

Your hamster will prefer to live somewhere quiet.

Make sure cats and other pets can't reach the cage.

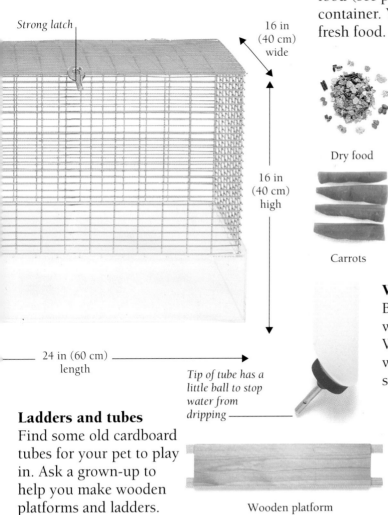

Strong latch

16 in (40 cm) wide

16 in (40 cm) high

24 in (60 cm) length

Water bottle

Buy a water bottle with a dropper. Water is let out when a hamster sucks the tube.

Tip of tube has a little ball to stop water from dripping

Your pet will get too hot near a radiator or in bright sunlight.

Your pet needs 12 hours of light and 12 hours of dark a day.

Ladders and tubes

Find some old cardboard tubes for your pet to play in. Ask a grown-up to help you make wooden platforms and ladders. These things will make your hamster's home more interesting.

Wooden platform

Ramp

Tube with footholds

Cardboard tube

Ladder

Other things you will need

You will need to get some special equipment to help you care for your new pet. You can find some of it at home; other things you will have to buy. Everything should be good quality, so it will last a long time. Make sure all the equipment is ready before you pick up your hamster.

Carrying box

Ask your vet for a carrying box in which to bring your hamster home. It should have plenty of small holes to let in fresh air.

Cleaning equipment

To clean your hamster's cage, you will need some special equipment. You can get safe disinfectant from your local vet's office. Keep all the cleaning supplies together so they are not used to clean anything else.

Dustpan

Brush

Rubber gloves

Dish washing liquid

Disinfectant spray

Spout brush

Scrubbing brush

Small scraper

Bottle brush

Health care

Find an old, small kitchen scale for when you weigh your hamster (see p. 43). Get a toothbrush to brush your pet's fur.

Bowl

Cleaning cloth

Toothbrush

Small scale

Handling equipment

Hamsters are very wriggly. To help you hold and look at your pet, make a wire grid (see p. 42) and a handling can from an old bottle (see p. 31).

Handling can

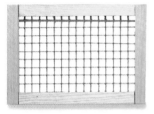

Wire grid

Catching kit

You will need a bucket, ramp, and towel to catch your hamster if it escapes (see p. 31).

Towel

Bucket

Wood ramp

The hamsterlarium

You can make your hamster's cage into a more natural home by replacing the tray with a burrowing tank (see p. 36). Syrian hamsters particularly like to burrow as they dig homes underground in the wild.

Hamster wonderland

By linking a few tanks together with tubes, you can make an amazing hamster home.

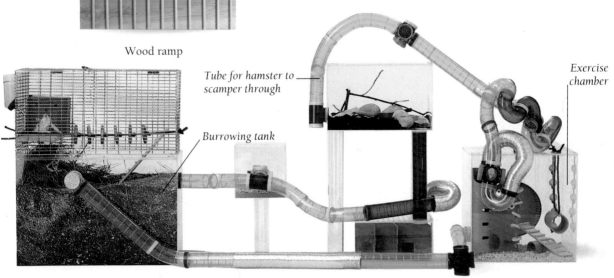

Exercise chamber

Tube for hamster to scamper through

Burrowing tank

Choosing a hamster

You can choose a baby hamster, called a puppy, from a litter when it is at least four weeks old. An adult hamster will also make a good pet. You can only keep one Syrian hamster in a cage, so if you want to keep two hamsters, choose dwarfs or Chinese.

Where to find your new hamster
- A friend's hamster may have baby hamsters.
- A breeder will sell you a breed of hamster.
- An animal shelter may have a hamster.

Getting a Syrian
A Syrian hamster likes to live on its own. It may fight another hamster that comes too close. If you want a Syrian, choose one male or one female.

Pair of Russians

Two Chinese hamsters

Mother Syrian hamster is held by the owner

Point to the baby Syrian that you like

Choosing Chinese or dwarfs
Dwarf hamsters live in pairs. Pet Chinese hamsters also like company. Unless you want your pets to breed, get two Chinese or Russians of the same sex from the same litter.

1 **When you go to choose** a puppy, ask to see the mother to be sure she is healthy. Don't touch any of the puppies at first. Now is the time to ask any questions.

2 **Look carefully** at all the puppies. If they are awake they will be scurrying around the tank. Ask the owner to pick up the hamster that seems liveliest. The owner may show it to you on a wire grid.

Puppy grips onto the wire grid

Wire bridge for puppies to cross

Nest box for puppies to sleep in

One puppy sits in the food bowl!

Look to see if the puppy has clear eyes

Fur should be soft, smooth, and clean

3 **Examine the puppy** you have picked out. It should have bright eyes, and a clean nose and ears. The fur should be dry all over, including under its bottom.

Put the puppy in the box bottom-first

4 **Ask the owner** to help you put the puppy you want in a carrying box lined with shredded paper. If you have decided to keep dwarfs or Chinese, you will need to choose another puppy of the same sex from the same litter.

Welcome home

Your hamster may be frightened when it leaves its brothers and sisters to go to your home. To help it settle in, have everything prepared in the cage. Make sure you have washed the cage and feeding equipment. You can visit your vet's office on the way home. Your vet will check that your hamster is healthy.

1 Fill the tray with wood shavings after lining it with paper. The paper will soak up urine. Your pet will burrow in the shavings.

Pile shavings to the top

Scoop the wood shavings from your storage bin

2 Put some shredded paper into the sleeping box. Your hamster will burrow into it to make a cozy nest. You can place pieces of paper towel in the cage. Your pet will tear them up to add to its bed.

3 Fix the water bottle to the side above a platform. Arrange the platforms, tubes, and ladders to make the cage as interesting as you can.

Sleeping box

Paper towel will be shredded

Rod to hang food from

Attach the water bottle with the wire

Slide the door open to put in the paper

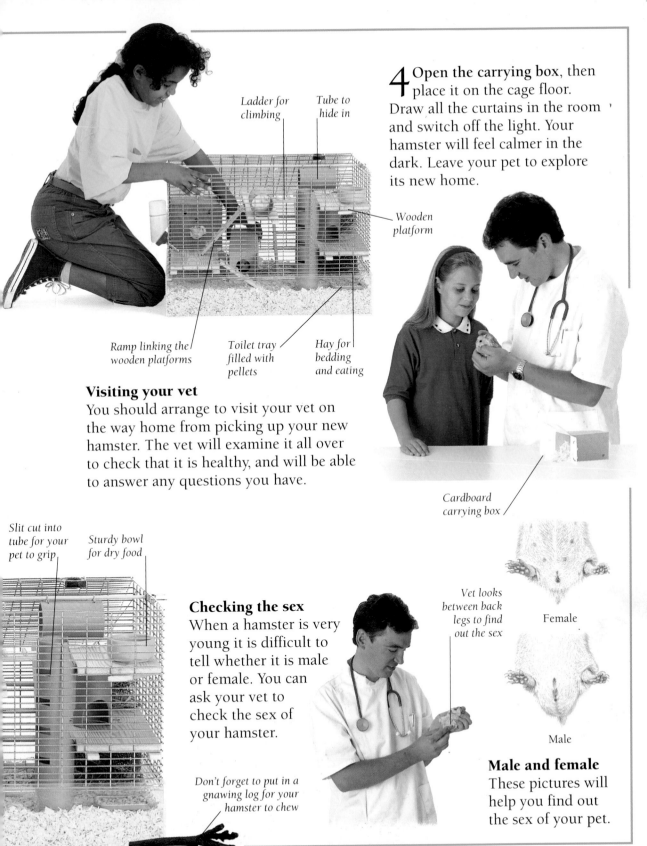

Ladder for climbing

Tube to hide in

4 **Open the carrying box**, then place it on the cage floor. Draw all the curtains in the room and switch off the light. Your hamster will feel calmer in the dark. Leave your pet to explore its new home.

Wooden platform

Ramp linking the wooden platforms

Toilet tray filled with pellets

Hay for bedding and eating

Visiting your vet
You should arrange to visit your vet on the way home from picking up your new hamster. The vet will examine it all over to check that it is healthy, and will be able to answer any questions you have.

Cardboard carrying box

Slit cut into tube for your pet to grip

Sturdy bowl for dry food

Vet looks between back legs to find out the sex

Female

Checking the sex
When a hamster is very young it is difficult to tell whether it is male or female. You can ask your vet to check the sex of your hamster.

Male

Don't forget to put in a gnawing log for your hamster to chew

Male and female
These pictures will help you find out the sex of your pet.

Feeding your hamster

Hamsters are omnivores, which means that they eat plants and other animals. In the wild, they eat seeds, plant roots and shoots, as well as insects, earthworms, and even mice. To keep your hamster fit, you must give it special hamster food and fresh fruit and vegetables (see pp. 28-29).

Razor sharp front teeth bite off portions of food

Mouth made for chewing
A hamster has 16 teeth that are a special shape for biting and grinding. Food is mixed with spit by the tongue while it is ground by the teeth.

Filling the pouches
It is hard for a wild hamster to find food. When it does, it stuffs its cheek pouches to carry the food home to store.

Making the hoard
When the hamster returns home, it empties its pouches by rubbing its cheeks with both front paws. Fresh food is eaten immediately. Dry food is stored to be eaten another time.

All this food has been emptied from the pouches

Hamster strokes its cheek to push out food

A pet hamster also stuffs its pouches

Nut is shelled to store in pouch

Pour dry food from the airtight container

Staple diet
You should feed your pet an "all-in-one" or "complete" dry food specially made for hamsters. It contains dried plants and seeds.

Sunflower seeds

Oats

Vitamins and minerals

Peanuts

Flaked pea

Processed wheat

Barley

Alfalfa

Ground nut pellets

Beet pulp

Maize

When to feed your hamster
Feed your hamster every evening after you have cleaned the cage (see p. 32). Your pet likes to have food to eat whenever it wants to.

How much to feed

Fill the bowl to the top, and hide small amounts of dry food around the cage. If your hamster eats all the food in the bowl, and leaves the hidden food, put less food in the bowl and more around the cage.

Hamster sniffs the food before eating it

Wipe all around the bowl

Clearing away leftovers

Thoroughly clean the food bowl every evening. Take out any hidden food that your hamster hasn't found. If you notice that your pet is eating less than usual, call your vet for advice.

Eating droppings

Don't worry if you see your pet eating its own droppings – all types of hamsters do this. Your hamster's stomach cannot take all the nutrients from food the first time it eats it. So your pet hamster makes droppings, which it eats again.

Grinding down the teeth

Your pet's front teeth grow all the time. Wild hamsters gnaw wood and roots and that keeps their teeth short. Give your hamster a log to gnaw.

An untreated apple tree branch is best

Fresh water

Wild hamsters get most of the water they need from the fresh food. Your hamster eats a lot of dry food, so you must make sure that its water bottle is always full.

Tongue licks the tube tip to make the water flow

Feeding fresh foods

Eating salads and fresh fruit every day helps keep you healthy. These foods are full of nutrients. Your hamster also likes to eat fresh foods. Give it spare fruit and vegetables from the kitchen and collect wild plants. But be careful! Some wild plants are poisonous. Wash all fresh food before feeding it to your pet.

Lettuce is nibbled by the front teeth

Grass

Dandelion

How much fresh food to feed
Give your hamster half a handful of fresh food every day. If it eats it all, give it a little more the next day. Be careful not to give too much fresh food, or your pet will get an upset stomach.

Wild plant food
Look at the pictures. These plants are all safe for your hamster to eat. Always ask a grown-up to check a plant before you give it to your hamster.

✿ Food must be fresh
Fresh plants, fruit, and vegetables quickly become stale. Every morning, throw away any fresh food that hasn't been eaten. When you clean out the cage, remove any fresh food that your hamster has hoarded.

Plantain

Shepherd's purse

Clover

Crunchy vegetables

Every day, chop up some vegetables to give to your hamster. The pieces can be quite large because your pet will enjoy biting them. Your greengrocer may be able to give you suitable scraps. Make sure they are fresh.

Turnip

Peas

Rutabaga

Celery

Alfalfa

Broccoli

Lettuce

Carrot

Cucumber

Grapes

Apple

Favorite fruit

Do not peel or remove the seeds from the fruit that you give to your hamster. It will enjoy stripping the peel with its teeth and digging out the seeds with its nimble paws.

Banana

Strawberries

Melon

Fresh food smells strongly

When to feed fresh food

Give fresh food to your hamster every evening, at the same time as you feed it dry food.

Attach pieces of food with a clip

Hamster stretches up to get to the food

Hamster stands up on back legs

Hiding fresh food

Hang fresh food from the cage, and hide it in other places. Your pet will sniff it, and get plenty of exercise trying to reach it.

Handling your hamster

To begin with, your hamster is frightened of anyone except its mother, brothers, and sisters. The more time you spend with your pet, the more quickly it will learn to trust you. Start to tame it right away. Let it hear your voice and smell you. Your hamster will soon learn that you are its friend. Then you will be able to pick it up and play with it.

Food smell attracts your pet to your hand

Hamster sniffs the food

Hand-feeding
Offer your hamster some fresh food from your hand. It will not run away because it will smell the food and want to eat it. It will soon become used to your big hand being close to it.

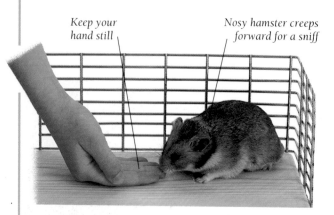

Keep your hand still

Nosy hamster creeps forward for a sniff

Sniffing your hand
Once your pet eats happily from your hand, let it sniff you. Put one hand down flat, keeping your fingers together.

Picking up your hamster
When your hamster is used to your smell, you can pick it up. Always make sure it is fully awake. Let it sniff your hand before you lift it. If your hands are small, pick it up in cupped hands.

Tuck your three middle fingers under the bottom

Hamster feels securely held

Put your little finger and thumb around the chest

Handling your pet

This chart tells you when to handle your new pet during the first two weeks.

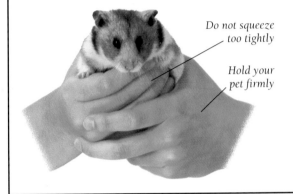

Do not squeeze too tightly

Hold your pet firmly

Day 1: Watch your pet, but don't disturb it.

Day 2: Start to hand-feed your hamster. Pick it up in your handling can. Talk to it quietly so it gets used to your voice.

Days 3 to 5: Pick up your pet in your hand.

Days 6 to 14: Put your hamster on its wire grid (see pp. 42-43). Brush your hamster. Introduce it to your family.

After 2 Weeks: Play with your pet several times a day.

Hamster climbs the ramp to look for the food it can smell

Bucket is lined with a towel

Walking from hand to hand

Once your hamster is used to being picked up, it will walk across your hands. If you keep putting one hand in front of the other, your hamster will keep on walking.

Hold your hands close to your chest

Catching your hamster

If your pet escapes, put a ramp and bucket with some food in a dark corner. Your pet will be tempted into the bucket by the food, but can't get out again.

Always sit when you hold your pet

The handling can

If at first you are afraid to pick up your pet, make a handling can out of an old plastic bottle. Only carry your pet in it for a few minutes.

Cleaning the cage

Your hamster likes its home to be very clean. If the cage gets dirty, your hamster may become ill. Every evening before feeding your pet, check the hoard, tidy the cage, clean the toilet tray, and wash the feeding equipment. Clean the whole cage thoroughly at least once a week.

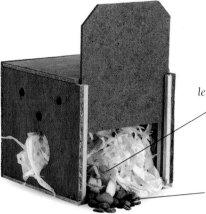

Remove lettuce and apple

Leave a little pile of seeds and nuts

1 **Open the sleeping box** to check your pet's "pantry." Slide the door gently so the hoard is not moved. Take away fresh food, but leave a small pile of the dried food.

2 **Take out the food bowl** and unclip the water bottle. Wipe the bowl with your cloth. Wash and rinse the water bottle before pouring in fresh water.

Use the spout brush to clean the metal tube

Scrub the water bottle with the bottle brush

Keep checking where your hamster is so it doesn't escape

Old cardboard tubes should be replaced

Clear away old food

3 **Put fresh litter** in the litter tray. Wash and dry the tray before you refill it. Put a bit of old litter on top, so your hamster recognizes its toilet tray.

Use the scoop to pour litter into the tray

4 **Take out chewed-up cardboard tubes** and dirty paper. Throw away old hay and scoop out soiled wood shavings. Try not to disturb the cage too much.

Rubber gloves keep hands dry

1 **Once a week**, empty everything out of the cage. Scrape off the lining paper. Save some of the hoard, shavings, and bedding. Put these back into the cage when you refill it, so your pet will feel at home.

Put your hamster into a bucket to keep it safe

Small pile of old wood shavings kept separate

Pull out all the bedding from the sleeping box

Bedding saved from sleeping box

Small bundle of shredded paper

Dried food from the "pantry"

Mound of soiled wood shavings can be thrown away

Make sure your cloth is not too wet

2 **Scrub the bottom** and sides of the tray with hot, soapy water. Dry the tray with paper towel. Spray the inside with special disinfectant. Leave the tray to air before refilling it.

Scrub hard to remove all the stains

Dish washing liquid

Dustpan and brush to sweep up

Special disinfectant kills germs

3 **Wipe the platforms** and the bars with a soapy cloth after sweeping away old food and bedding. Take out the ladder and ramps to clean them. Then wipe everything with a cloth soaked in clean water.

33

Understanding your hamster

Your hamster shows its moods by moving parts of its body. It marks the things that belong to it with its scent. It pulls in its paws to its body when it is frightened. When you see it standing up it is usually curious but it may be angry. Watch your pet closely, and you will soon understand what it is doing. You will also see how it spends its time: exercising, sleeping, and burrowing.

Sniffing for clues
Your pet twitches its nose to sniff its surroundings. It pushes its nose against the ground to smell for food.

Marking what's mine
Just like you, your hamster labels the things that it owns. Instead of writing its name on them, it leaves its scent. The scent is in the skin around the eyes, ears, and bottom. In Syrian hamsters, the scent is also in the grease from the hip spots.

Hip spot lets out a smelly grease

Hamster makes itself tall by stretching up

Rolling in surprise
If your hamster is disturbed by a sudden movement or is woken up quickly, it leans over on one side. It pulls its head down toward its body to show that it is scared.

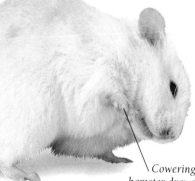

Cowering hamster draws in its paws

Eye opens wide to stare

On the lookout
When your pet is interested in something it has heard or smelled, it lifts a paw off the ground. It may stand up to make itself look big and bold while it looks around.

Front paw is raised

Hamster balances on hind legs

Good grooming

You will see your hamster spend a lot of time grooming itself. It uses its front paws as washcloths and its sharp teeth to nibble through tangled fur. The claws on its back legs make fine combs.

Rough tongue scrapes off dirt

Hamster bends to reach back leg

Animal acrobat

Watch your hamster enjoy itself exploring and playing with the things in its cage. It has a very good sense of balance. A simple rope ladder will help keep it happy and fit.

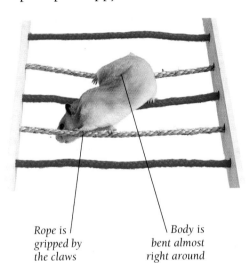

Rope is gripped by the claws

Body is bent almost right around

Fast asleep

Your pet sleeps for about 14 hours every day. It keeps itself warm by curling up in a ball. If the weather is very cold, a Syrian hamster may sleep deeply for several days.

Head is drawn into body

Eye is firmly closed

Busy burrower

A pet hamster needs to burrow as much as a wild hamster. You will often see your pet digging a tunnel in its bedding or litter with its front paws. Try to figure out where the tunnel will come out.

Hamster pokes its head out of a tunnel

Eye stares out curiously

Soft wood shavings are easy to burrow in

Things to do with your pet

Look in magazines about pets, or ask at your vet's office, for the address of your local hamster club. After you join, you can enter your pet in competitions to find the best cared-for hamster. You will meet other hamster owners who will tell you how to make interesting things for your pet. It is easy to attach a burrowing tank filled with hay, peat, and wood shavings to the cage. This is called a hamsterlarium. You can also make an exercise wheel to help your pet keep fit.

Large wheel is fixed to the back of the cage

Large exercise wheel
Your hamster needs to run a long way every day to stay healthy. Buy or make a solid exercise wheel, rather than one with open rungs. Your pet can run as far as it likes without leaving its cage or hamsterlarium.

Add the wood shavings with your scoop

Small tank filled with litter pellets

Short pieces of hay

Wheel is made from the bottom of a large plastic bucket

Corrugated board lines the wheel for grip

Peat

Making a hamsterlarium
Make a burrowing tank out of an aquarium. Make sure it is the right size for the cage to fit securely on top. Fill half the tank with peat. Add cut-up hay and wood shavings. Mix everything together.

The finished hamsterlarium

Fix the cage to the top of the burrowing tank. Attach the wheel to the metal bars. Half-bury a container filled with pellets for your hamster to use as a toilet. Now is a good time to redesign the inside of the cage.

Coconut shell filled with dried food

Multi-colored rope walkway

Peat, hay, and wood shavings are well mixed

Tunnel has been dug in peat by the hamster

Hamster gnaws on a small piece of wood

Leaving your pet

Going on vacation
You can't always take your pet with you when you go on vacation. You must find someone to look after it. You may have a friend with a hamster who can look after your pet as well.

Making a checklist
Make a list of the jobs that need doing every day. Write them down in the order you do them. Your hamster may be upset if the usual order is changed. Make a note of the name and telephone number of your vet.

What to pack
Get all of your pet equipment ready for your friend. Make sure that you pack enough food, bedding, and litter. Don't forget all the cleaning and handling things. Remind your friend to get fresh food to feed your pet every day.

Moving your hamster
Take the cage and your pet in its carrying box to your friend. Your friend will need to play with your pet out of its cage every day. Tell her to be careful that it doesn't escape.

A hamster wonderland

In the wild, a hamster makes a burrow with different rooms. It runs through the tunnels and comes to the surface to search for food. You can make a copy of this wild home by linking cages and tanks together with tubes. Buy and make equipment to create this wonderland in stages—you don't need to build it all at once. Remember not to leave any gaps through which your pet can escape.

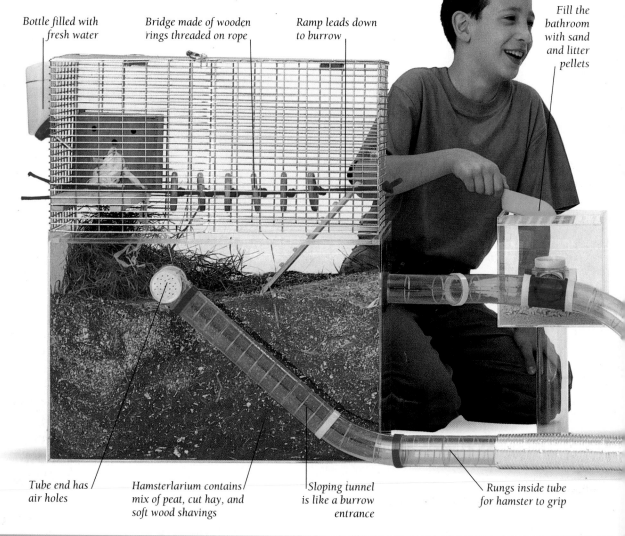

Bottle filled with fresh water

Bridge made of wooden rings threaded on rope

Ramp leads down to burrow

Fill the bathroom with sand and litter pellets

Tube end has air holes

Hamsterlarium contains mix of peat, cut hay, and soft wood shavings

Sloping tunnel is like a burrow entrance

Rungs inside tube for hamster to grip

Adding each room

Begin your hamster's wonderland with the hamsterlarium. Buy tanks and turn them into an exercise room, a bathroom, a maze, and an outside area. Connect the rooms with tubes. Line the bathroom with litter, the exercise room with wood shavings, and the outside area with peat and rocks. Fill each room with cardboard and wooden objects for your pet to explore.

Put fresh food in the outside area

Hamster runs toward the outside area as it smells the fresh food

Twisting tubes are fun for hamster to scurry through

Bowl filled with dry food

Outside area with peat, rocks, and branches

Large exercise room

Wooden ball and rope ladder

Entrance to exercise room

Exercise wheel

Tube swing

Cardboard maze

Vertical escape tunnel leads to maze

Tube with slits to climb down

Wooden ring ladder

Wooden seesaw

Having babies

 Just as grown-up women can have children, female hamsters can have babies, called puppies. Think very carefully before putting a male and a female hamster together. They will probably fight. They may breed. If you do let your hamsters breed, you will have to find homes for as many as 14 puppies.

1 **Newborn puppies** are very small and have no fur. They can't see or hear; they can only smell. They pull themselves along by their front feet. If a puppy strays from the nest, the mother will carry it back in her mouth.

Eye is not yet open

🐾 Responsible ownership
It may seem like fun to let your female hamster have puppies. But don't forget that these cuddly balls of fluff quickly grow up. Each of the puppies will need a separate home.

Mother carries the baby in her mouth

Puppies huddle together for warmth

2 **At two weeks**, the puppies have soft, furry coats. They drink milk from their mother, which gives them the nutrients they need to grow.

Puppy scrambles to drink

Ear picks up sounds

Eye is now open

Coat is soft and fluffy

Nose twitches to sniff new surroundings

Puppy stays near its brothers and sisters

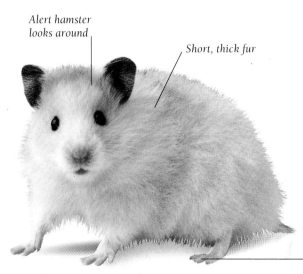

Alert hamster looks around

Short, thick fur

3 **The puppies leave** their mother after three weeks. They play together to learn how to look after themselves, and hardly ever fight. They eat dry and fresh food and begin to make hoards. The puppies burrow tunnels in their bedding and litter.

Tube for hamster to climb up

Feet have fully grown claws

Hamster pokes its head out of a tube

Slit in tube for hamster to grip

4 **A five-week-old hamster** is ready to live on its own. If a Syrian hamster is kept with its brothers and sisters, it will fight them viciously. A female is now old enough to have puppies of her own.

5 **A hamster is almost fully grown** at four months. It is active and energetic. It likes to explore its surroundings. It will enjoy having many interesting things to play with in its cage.

Health care

You need to care for your hamster properly to make sure it stays healthy. You must give it the right kind of food (see p. 26), clean its cage out regularly (p. 32), and keep its coat well groomed. You also need to do simple health checks with your hamster every day. You will learn to spot quickly if your hamster is ill. If you think something is wrong, call your vet for advice immediately.

Brush back the fur so you can see the skin

1 **Put your hamster on the grid** to look at it closely. Make sure it is alert and not limping. Push back the fur—it should feel soft and smell clean all over.

Look down the ear hole

2 **Examine your hamster's ears** by pulling back each ear flap. They should be clean and not smell. Check your pet's eyes. They should be bright and shiny.

Gently push back the flap

3 **Hold your pet** in one hand and gently pull back its lips with the thumb and first finger of your other hand. Look at the teeth. They should be short and sharp.

Healthy hamster teeth are yellow and white

Don't grip too tightly

Carefully squeeze the paw to show the claws

Claw is the right length

Claw is too long

4 **Check the claws** on each paw. Hold each of your hamster's tiny feet between your thumb and first finger. Look to see that the claws are the correct length.

Line the tray with paper towel

Weighing your pet
Weigh your hamster at the same time, on the same day, every week. Write down the result. If your hamster has lost or gained weight, it may be ill, or it may not be getting enough exercise.

Grooming a long-hair
A long-haired hamster should be groomed every day. Brush the coat with a toothbrush. Blow wood shavings off the fur. Carefully untangle any knots with the tips of your fingers.

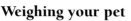

Stroke with the brush away from the head

Wood shavings are caught in the long hair

Your pet care checklist
Use this list to keep a record of all the jobs you need to do.

Copy this chart. Check off the jobs when you have finished them.

Every day:
Feed your pet
Wash the bowls
Wash and fill bottle
Check the hoard
Tidy bedding
Clean litter tray
Handle your hamster
Groom your pet
Look at the coat
Check eyes and ears
Examine claws
Check teeth length

◆

Once a week:
Scrub out the cage
Weigh your hamster
Check food and bedding supplies

◆

Once a month:
Rearrange the cage

◆

Every year:
Take your hamster to the vet for a full checkup

Visiting the veterinarian

The veterinarians who work at your local vet's office know a lot about hamsters. They want to help you keep your hamster happy and healthy. They will tell you how to care for your pet properly. You can ask them as many questions as you like. They will also try to make your pet better if it becomes ill.

Veterinary assistant is happy to answer your questions

Your veterinarian

Your vet gives your hamster special health checks. If your pet is ill, she will tell you what needs to be done to make it better. She may give you medicine for your hamster, or ask you to care for it in a special way.

Your veterinary assistant

Telephone the veterinary assistant at your vet's office if you want to find out more about your hamster or are worried that it is ill. The assistant may suggest that you and your hamster come to see the vet.

Take your hamster's cage to the vet so she can check it

A stethoscope is used to hear a hamster's heartbeat

White coat keeps the vet clean

Take your pet to the vet in its carrying box

My pet's fact sheet

Try making a fact sheet about your pet hamster. Copy the headings on this page, or you can make up your own! Then write in the correct information about your hamster.

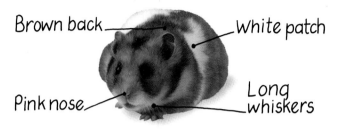

Brown back   White patch

Pink nose   Long whiskers

Leave a space to stick in a photograph or draw a picture of your hamster. Then label all of your pet's special features.

Name: **Alice**

Birthday: **January 16th**

Weight: **3½ oz. (100g)**

Favorite fresh food: **Lettuce**

Best game: **Climbing ladders**

Veterinarian's name: **Mark Evans**

Vet's office telephone number: **555-1234**

Index